CW01022105

Panoramas *of* Portugal

A TRAVEL PHOTO ART BOOK

LAINE CUNNINGHAM

Panoramas of Portugal
A Travel Photo Art Book

Published by Sun Dogs Creations
Changing the World One Book at a Time
Softcover ISBN: 9781946732491
Hardcover ISBN: 9781946732507

Cover Design by Angel Leya

Introduction

Portugal has a long and varied history. After being invaded and settled by groups as old as the Pre-Celts and the Romans, struggles continued with Visigoths and other Germanic people. In 711 CE, the nation was firmly established.

Portugal is perhaps best known for being the first truly global empire. Its maritime exploration during the early part of the Age of Discovery, the 15th and 16th centuries, provided an influx of wealth through the spice trade. The Joanine era saw more than spices ship through her ports. Gold, wheat, copperware, cloths, tools, wine, and horses were all traded.

Then came centuries of turmoil. From the 17th through the 19th centuries, wars, the loss of colonies, and a lack of participation in the Industrial Revolution saw the nation decline. Then a significant earthquake triggered destruction, fires, and a tsunami that almost completely destroyed Lisbon.

Today Portugal is a striking place for tourism with unique architecture, a sunny climate, and Mediterranean culture. The cuisine is renowned, and fresh seafood spiced with chili and black peppers, saffron and olive oil can be found at inexpensive restaurants. Wander through this astonishing place with *Panoramas of Portugal*.

UPWARD MOBILITY

DREAMING JOURNEY

FRAGMENTED

CRUISE SHIP

CREATION

BISHOPS

PLUNGE

NETTLE WIND

WHIRLIGIGS

TUBEWAY

PINKING SHEARS

FAITHFUL

BREEZEWAY

CORNER OFFICE

KEEPING WATCH

TARGET

SURVEILLANCE

STARING SKY

WEDDING CAKE

SAILING

GRAPH PAPER

LUNCH WITH ALIENS

GARDEN WALL

PLAYPEN

PROUD PIG

BLUE MOOD

BREACHING

RUBICUND

CUPS OF BOUNTY

LONGHOUSE

A SIMPLE COTTAGE

SEMAPHORE

QAL'EH RAFTEN

SLEEPING WOMAN

BRIGHT TIERS

FAIRYTALE

About the Author

Laine Cunningham leads readers around the world. *The Family Made of Dust* is set in the Australian Outback, while *Reparation* is a novel of the American Great Plains. Her travel memoir *Woman Alone* appeals to fans of *Wild* and *Eat Pray Love*.

Novels by
Laine Cunningham

The Family Made of Dust

Beloved

Reparation

Other Books by
Laine Cunningham

Woman Alone: A Six-Month Journey
Through the Australian Outback

On the Wallaby Track

Seven Sisters: Spiritual Messages from Aboriginal Australia

Writing While Female or Black or Gay

The Zen of Travel
The Zen of Gardening
Zen in the Stable
The Zen of Chocolate
The Zen of Dogs

Ruins of Rome I & II
Ancients of Assisi I & II
Panoramas of Portugal
Nuances of New York
Glimpses of Germany
Impressions of Italy
Altitudes of the Alps
Coast of California
Flourishes of France
Portraits of Paris
Tableaus of Tbilisi
Grandeur in the Republic of Georgia
Paragons of Prague
Hidden Prague
Lidice Lives
Along the Via Appia
The Pillars of the Bohemian Paradise
Terezín and Theresienstadt
Garden City Garbatella
Captivating Capri
Notre Dame Cathedral
The Beauty of Berlin
Milan Cathedral
Treasures of Turin

The Wisdom of Puppies
The Wisdom of Babies
The Wisdom of Weddings

The Beautiful Book of Questions
The Beautiful Book for Dream Seekers
The Beautiful Book for Rebels
The Beautiful Book for Women
The Beautiful Book for Lovers